Working Scientifically

FINDING INFORMATION AND MAKING ARGUMENTS

by Riley Flynn

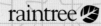

raintree
a Capstone company — publishers for children

Raintree is an imprint of Capstone Global Library Limited, a company incorporated in England and Wales having its registered office at 264 Banbury Road, Oxford, OX2 7DY – Registered company number: 6695582

www.raintree.co.uk
myorders@raintree.co.uk

Edited by Anna Butzer
Designed by Sarah Bennett
Picture research by Eric Gohl
Production by Laura Manthe

Printed and bound in China.
ISBN 978 1 4747 2257 5
20 19 18 17 16
10 9 8 7 6 5 4 3 2 1

British Library Cataloguing in Publication Data
A full catalogue record for this book is available from the British Library.

Acknowledgements
Capstone: 9, 11; Shutterstock: Becky Sheridan, 17, Ivan Kuzmin, 19, Kdonmuang, 7, kozzi, 20, Monkey Business Images, 13, overcrew, 15, PointImages, 5, wavebreakmedia, cover
Design Elements: Shutterstock

Contents

Think like a scientist

Scientists look for information to understand our world. Information helps them to test ideas and solve problems. To think like a scientist, you need to look for information.

Where can you find information?
You can read a book or
an online article. You can also
watch a video about a topic.
Information is all around us.

Use text features

Text features can help you find key information. Start by reading the contents page. Then look for headings, bold print and text boxes.

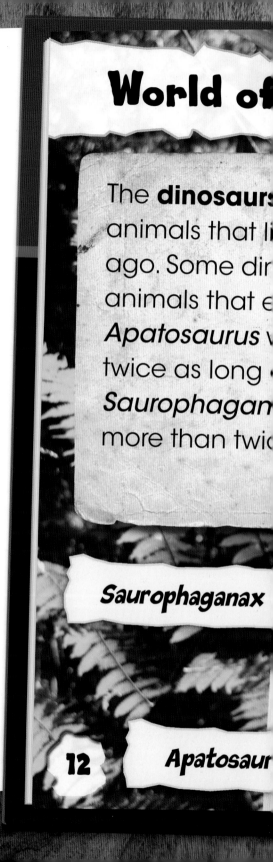

World of

The **dinosaur**
animals that li
ago. Some din
animals that e
Apatosaurus v
twice as long
Saurophagan
more than twic

Saurophaganax

12   *Apatosaur*

ants

re a group of
millions of years
urs were the biggest
walked on Earth.
23 metres long, about
bus. The hunter
was 11 metres long,
s long as a car.

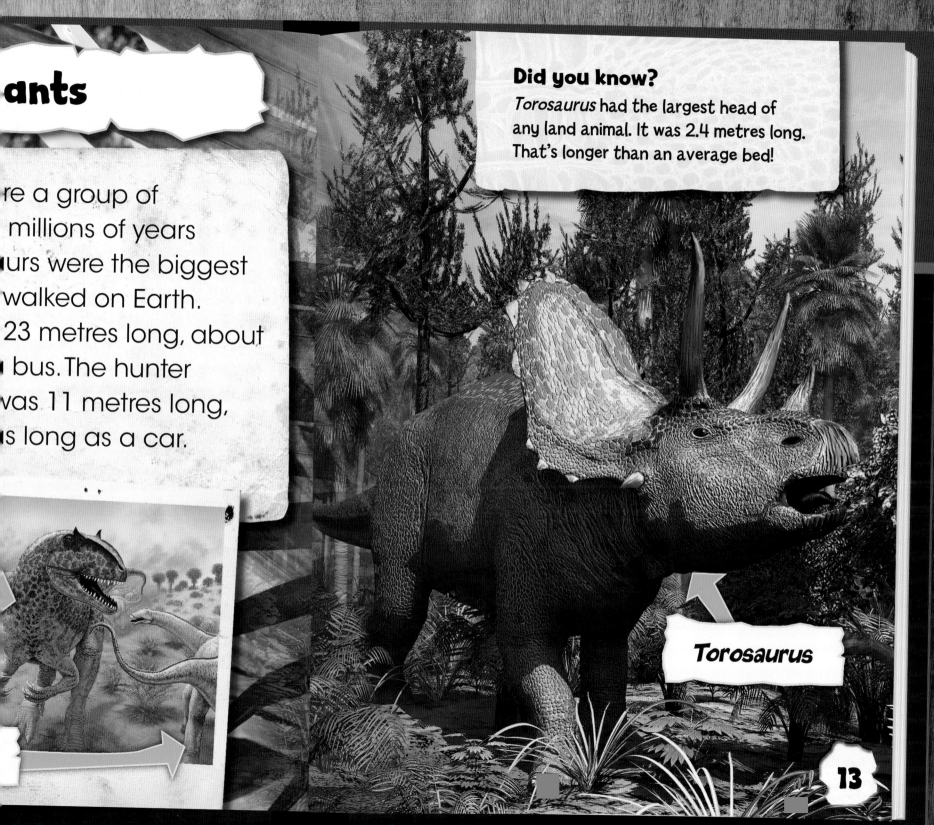

Torosaurus

13

Pictures also hold information.

You are reading about dinosaurs.

What do the different dinosaurs

look like? Do the pictures have

labels? These features help you

to understand the text.

The long

One of the lon
sauropod calle
to be 27 metre
than the length
Sauropods live
animals walked
they could be
older dinosaurs

14 *Diplodocu*

k

dinosaurs was a
Diplodocus. It grew
ng. That is longer
a swimming pool.
herds. The younger
the centre where
ected by the larger,

Did you know?
Some sauropods, such as
Saltasaurus, had bone **armour**
on their backs to protect them
from attack.

Saltasaurus

15

Facts and evidence

Gathering information helps you to build an argument. To argue about a topic you need to know facts. We can prove a fact to be true.

Arguments need facts. You may say that we should not throw rubbish into a river. Why not? Fish may think the rubbish is food. Our rubbish can harm fish. That is a fact.

Every argument also has two parts. The first part is a claim. The claim is the main point. You can claim that some animals see well in the dark.

The second part of an argument is evidence. You have observed bats flying and eating in the dark. This evidence proves your claim.

Finding information and making claims

Which food will attract the most insects at a picnic? Find out!

What you need:

- pencil
- paper
- honey
- bread
- hot dog, cut up into small pieces
- 3 jam jar lids
- ruler
- timer, clock or watch
- a dry or sunny day

What to do:

1. Draw three columns on the piece of paper.
   List the items of food – one in each column.

2. Place a small amount of each food on a jam
   jar lid. Put the lids outside. Place the lids about
   10 centimetres apart.

3. Observe the lids. Write down the time you start
   watching the lids.

4. Each time an insect inspects a food, draw a tick in
   its column. Also write down the type of insect.

5. How long did it take for each food to attract its
   first insect? Add this information to each column.

What do you think now?

Make a claim. A claim is something you believe to
be true. Which type of food will attract the most
insects at a picnic? Why? Now share what you have
learned with a friend.

Glossary

argument set of reasons to support an idea

claim say that something is true

evidence information that helps to prove something is true or false

fact information that is truthful and correct

gather collect things

label word or phrase that describes something

observe watch someone or something closely in order to learn about it

problem something that raises questions

Read more

365 Science Activities (Usborne Activities),
(Usborne Publishing, 2014)

Experiments with Light (Read and Experiment),
Isabel Thomas (Raintree, 2015)

Websites

www.bbc.co.uk/bitesize/ks1/science
Enjoy some fun activities and learn more about
science.

www.dkfindout.com/uk/science
Find out more about science and famous scientists.

Comprehension questions

1. What is a fact?

2. Look at the pictures on pages 9 and 11. What text features can you see?

Index